The Chemo Conqueror: A Step-By-Step Guide To Building A Bulletproof Mindset During Treatment

The Bridge Between Chemotherapy And Mental Health.

George Davies

Copyright © 2024 by George Davies

All rights reserved. No part of this book may be reproduced, distributed, or transmitted in any form or by any means, without the prior written permission of the author, except in the case of brief quotations embodied in critical reviews and certain other non-commercial uses permitted by copyright law.

ISBN: 978-1-0686816-0-8

TikTok- @gdchat

Contents

Introduction 1

SMART Goals 9

Exercise 14

Food 17

Studying 20

Journalling 22

Plan For The Future 24

Learn A New Skill 26

Keep A Good Routine 28

Do Not Shut Off From The People Around You 31

Books And Podcasts 34

Manifestation 37

Be Kind To Yourself 40

Embrace The Change In Mindset 42

Step Out Of Your Comfort Zone 44

Schedule Worry Time 46

The 10-Minute Rule 48

Meditation, Gratitude, Positive Affirmations And Mantras 50

ASMR 53

The Relaxation Bundle 55

Learn To Live In The Moment 59

A Fresh Start Filled With New Opportunities 61

Be Selfish And Do What Makes You Happy 63

Pleasure And Mastery 65

Tough Times Make Funny Stories 68

Mental Health 74

Life After Cancer 82

Farewell (For Now) 88

Introduction

I've thought long and hard about my aim and how I want to introduce this book. If you're looking for scientific research with case studies and statistics to back it up, you'll find an abundance of those elsewhere, written by professionals. Instead, I envisioned this book as your trusted companion, a relatable friend with some experience who can steer you in the right direction. This right here is my chemo-conquering creation, using my story to help you build a bulletproof routine during and after your treatment. What I want to share with you is not complex in any way. However, I believe these tips and tricks can be the building blocks of something special. I want you to stand face to face with cancer and say **I will not be stopped**.

When I first started chemotherapy, I did not know which way to turn. I felt like my entire life had been stripped away, and my routine had been obliterated. My initial response was to bury my head in the sand and hope that the problem would resolve itself, a coping mechanism I had turned to in the past. Yet, experience had shown me that this approach rarely led to favourable outcomes. Five years ago, I had hit rock bottom, I was a heavy-smoking, morbidly obese alcoholic, completely consumed by depression and anxiety. I couldn't even leave the house without alcohol in my system. I would drink vodka for breakfast, rise and moonshine as I liked to call it, in a poor attempt at humour to mask the pain of my life falling apart. I gambled away every penny I had on slot machines because I believed that I only had two options left in life. Become rich enough to hide away in the comfort of my own home, or simply not be here anymore. There is so much more to that part of my life, However, we will save that for another time and get back to the matter at hand.

For the last few years, I have worked tirelessly on improving myself: losing weight, ditching cigarettes, and gaining control of excessive drinking and gambling. I am eternally grateful that I was able to work on myself and learn these valuable lessons before I was diagnosed with cancer. I dread to think how George from five years ago would've coped with this. I knew shutting off was no longer an option, one of the most valuable lessons I learned was how to not feel like a burden to the people around me anymore. You do not need to face cancer alone; **you are not a burden.** Sharing my journey with my family, the wonderful nurses (shout out to Yazmin, Abbie and all the incredible haematology department at Northampton General

Hospital) and on TikTok all made the entire process more manageable, a problem shared is a problem halved.

This book embodies what I wish I had when I first embarked on this journey, I aim to share realistic strategies and ideas that I used to stay motivated, in a time when it was very easy to slip into the abyss. Now, I am not saying that every piece of advice I give will resonate with everybody who reads this. I'm sure there will be a few eye rolls and thoughts of despair from some, as I waffle on about certain topics that do not interest them in the slightest, and that's okay. Having said that, I guarantee that if you begin to incorporate even a few of these into your day, you will reap the rewards. I've began to develop a real passion for coaching and helping others, therefore, I wanted to also provide you with the techniques I have picked up from my learning in this field, that have aided me through chemotherapy and radiotherapy. I have conducted the research for you and then simplified it to your advantage, because you don't need any unnecessary hassle right now, as I know only too well. One thing I want to make crystal clear is that I completely understand everybody's time through cancer treatment will be different. A plethora of factors will determine how badly somebody is affected: the type of cancer, the stage of the cancer, age, lifestyle and many more will dictate the severity of the treatment and how well they are able to cope. I was fortunate enough to be diagnosed with a treatable blood cancer, therefore, I was able to focus on the positive aspect of that to keep me motivated and drive me through. Another positive I had going for me was my age, and the fact that I had managed to obtain a good level of health and fitness over the last few years, with a keen interest in exercise and nutrition being a welcomed bonus in this situation. I thoroughly believe that if I had been diagnosed with this illness five years ago, I would not have lived to tell the tale. My self-destructive lifestyle and complete neglect of my own wellbeing would've prevented me from any sort of fight against cancer. I'm sure I would've just accepted defeat and drank myself into oblivion, wallowing in self-pity. Luckily for me, this was no longer the case due to many of the skills and techniques listed in this book already being applied to my life. However, somebody reading this could be beginning treatment for a much more destructive cancer in a worse condition than myself. If you find yourself in a situation like this, then let me first just say that I will never claim to understand exactly what you are going through. However, I know I can relate to many aspects of the path you are about to venture down, and this advice that I'm providing you with will 100% help you through your battle.

The more I reflected on my past, the clearer it became that I have spent most of my life waiting around for somebody to come and rescue me from my miserable existence. As if a stranger was going to wave a magic wand and gift me a way out of my misery. Unfortunately, life does not operate that way, so I decided it was time to give myself a well-needed kick up the backside and begin my self-rescue mission, and I want you to come along with me. The unknown of such treatment can be very daunting and knowing where to start was the first problem on the agenda, which is what led to me writing this. I feel I could've benefitted from some realistic and personal guidance of what to expect, along with a few pointers on how to structure my day throughout this testing time of my life. Something to supply me with that little bit of hope, even when the days felt long, and the light at the end of the tunnel seemed so far away. Going through something as drastic as cancer can be a very lonely place, believe me, I know. So, if this book can help even just one person feel like they're not alone, or give them the tiniest bit of guidance, then it has more than served its purpose. So, if you're ready to take the fight against cancer, while listening to a few stories involving pooing in a dish and a visit to the sperm bank, then look no further; you are in for a treat.

So, let's go back to the beginning of my story; two weeks before my sister's wedding in July 2022 I discovered a lump above my collarbone. The first thing I did was try to deny all knowledge of it and pretend it didn't exist, as avoidance had been my go-to coping mechanism for my entire life so far. However, I knew this was beyond naïve when a lump was present, so I decided to get it checked out when I returned from Greece, and to my dismay, the lump had not magically disappeared. Now, I won't bore you with all the details of my diagnosis and the entire process of what I went through. I'll save that for another book as I'm sure if you're reading this, you're already all too familiar with how it plays out. We arrive at that all-important day, the one where you are sat face to face with your doctor, while they try to figure out the best possible way to break the news that your life is about to change, your freedom is gone, and there is nothing you can do about it. Sat in that room with the doctor and the cancer nurse, hearing that I was now a cancer boy was a day that I never thought would come. As cliché as it sounds, you never imagine it happening to you, and yet here we were.

I reacted as I imagine many others have in that scenario; I was numb with next to no emotion and at a loss for words. I knew this was now uncharted territory for me, what do I do now? It took a while to process my emotions. I spent the entire drive home in silence next to my Mum, feeling as though I had let her down, while 'Last Last' by Burna Boy sounded sorrowfully on the radio in the background.

Let's fast forward again to the start of chemotherapy; now I was signed off work, with no purpose to fulfil my day, and to tell you the truth, I was terrified. This was one of the hardest parts of chemotherapy for me, because I realised very quickly that I needed to create some sort of structure and routine, to prevent completely losing my sanity and hope. For the last few years of my life, I had been working very hard on myself both physically and mentally. I'd become quite a creature of habit with a strict routine of training in the gym around my work schedule. Now that these had both been taken away from me, I was left with a big void of guilt that I needed to fill by finding ways to keep myself feeling productive. I was beginning to try and put a positive spin on things, convincing myself that, of course, I had not asked for this time off, but now that I had been given it, I could potentially use it to my advantage and accomplish tasks that I would usually be too busy to do. This is where the list of activities begins, these are things that I found gave me some well-needed structure in a time of uncertainty and allowed me to stay in control of my emotions. Unfortunately, this advice is not a miraculous cure, and there will still be many challenges throughout this journey. But I believe these things genuinely helped to keep me out of a very dark place during one of the most challenging periods of my life. I think it's imperative to find a balance between productivity and self-care, remember that as rewarding as it is to be productive, you also need to be using this time to heal and recover as your body is going through a tremendous amount. Be kind to yourself.

The following tips helped me feel productive and allowed me to work on myself. I was constantly seeking ways to use this time to grow as a person. I aimed to acquire new skills and knowledge for when I was released back into the big bad world. I wanted a better chance of creating the life that I yearned for instead of going back to my dull and miserable existence, wishing the days away.

SMART Goals

My aim is to create some sort of simplified structure for your days during this difficult period, which I could've used when starting. I believe SMART goals are a very fitting place to begin. SMART stands for specific, measurable, achievable, relevant and time-bound. Basically, it's a very simple way of setting yourself a realistic goal that you can track along the way to ensure you achieve it. Too many times, we say to ourselves, 'I really want to do this' or 'I want to be good at that.' Then, two days later, we have completely forgotten what we set out to achieve, and the dream is dead before it has even begun. Taking the time at the start of your journey to physically write out your SMART goals will be incredibly beneficial. It will help set a purpose for your days because, believe me, they will be long and slow at times, and will allow you to reflect on your progress to see if you are moving in the right direction. For example, over the last few years I have lost a significant amount of weight. Five years ago, I was at an all-time low: very overweight, heavily reliant on alcohol and cigarettes, and basically just not taking care of myself at all. I decided to change all that and, thankfully, found a genuine love for running and the gym. It's fair to say that I am now utterly obsessed with my weight, calories, and all that comes with it. So, for me one of my biggest worries at the start of chemotherapy, as silly as it sounds, was if I was going to gain weight. I was absolutely petrified, so I decided to turn my fear into a SMART goal to help me keep on top of it while I was going through treatment. Let's break it down into different sections to give you a detailed example of how it works.

Specific- This part of my goal is setting out exactly what I want to achieve in a clear and precise manner, 'I want to keep my body weight between 70kg and 73kg at all times during chemotherapy'. This is a specific goal, straight to the point, conveying what I want to achieve in a short and defined sentence. I specified a lower weight as well because I knew during chemotherapy, it was just as important to not lose too much weight. Eating good quality nutritious foods, and keeping your strength up is potentially the most crucial part of this entire journey, which I will get to very soon. Therefore, I knew even with the dreaded fear of weight gain, I couldn't allow that to have the reverse effect on me.

Measurable- Now I have a specific goal that I want to achieve, I need to ensure I have a way to measure my progress at different stages. This means ensuring I have the correct tools to track my results and keep on top of my new goal. Of course, the obvious one for my goal would be using the measuring scales to keep an eye on my weight. I decided to complete a weekly weigh-in, always first thing in the morning on a Friday. This ensured it would be a fair reading every week, just before any danger of a little weekend binge which was always very possible.

Achievable- This part is self-explanatory, however crucial; the goal must be realistic and within reach. Linking back to my goal of target weight, if I had set myself the target of getting down to 60kg during my time through chemo, then my goal would no longer be achievable, along with being rather unhealthy. Setting such a goal would likely lead to demotivation and a sense of defeat before even beginning, making you more likely to throw the towel in, which I'm sure is a familiar feeling for most of us reading this. The trick is to find the sweet spot of making it achievable but also challenging enough to keep you engaged, allowing you to feel satisfied once you accomplish the goal. We want to challenge ourselves, not be overwhelmed (we'll leave the overwhelming to the cancer).

Relevant- Next on the list, I need to ensure the goal is relevant to my needs; my main focus was keeping healthy during my treatment and ensuring my weight didn't begin to creep back up. Having been a little 'porker' for the majority of my life, the PTSD was firmly kicking in at this point. Waking up in cold sweats as memories of consuming the average male's weekly calorie recommendation in one sitting, began to haunt my dreams. This being true meant that my goal of maintaining between 70-73kg during chemotherapy was very relevant. It was all about exactly what I wanted to achieve: maintaining a healthy weight for myself and keeping off that extra timber from my past.

Time-bound- The icing on the cake (food on the brain, typical George): I need to set myself a deadline to achieve my goal. Pressure is one of my least favourite things in this world; some people thrive, while I tend to sob silently in a dark room for a while. Having said that, it is crucial if we want to be productive with our goals. It is far too easy to put things off when we don't have a deadline and leave these problems for our future selves. We need a precise time frame to allow us to track our progress and show ourselves whether we have been successful with this goal. My time frame for this goal was, of course, until my treatment and mission were completed, so now it is time for me to set myself a new goal. It will be just as detailed as this one, covering all the aspects of the SMART goal principle, like I have done before to keep progressing and moving forward. Self-development is never-ending; we can always strive for more.

Exercise

My SMART goals example leads to my next point seamlessly: exercise can genuinely be one of the most powerful tools for a healthier mind. I know some of you may think that exercise is the devil even without the whole cancer debacle, believe me, I've been there. But one of the biggest pieces of advice I could give you from my personal experience is to **Move when you can.**

Treatment will be a rollercoaster; some days, you will feel horrendous and probably not want to even venture from your bed. At times, it can feel like some sort of infinite merry-go-round from which you cannot wait to get off. This is when you absolutely need to listen to your body and rest up. However, you will have better days in between, sudden bursts of motivation and urges to be useful, which I wholeheartedly believe you should take advantage of and get your body moving. I am not recommending you start training for marathons or lifting heavy weights, but I think low-impact exercise, such as walking, can be incredibly beneficial for your mind and body, at a time when both are taking a beating.

I found it very easy to convince myself at times that I was 'useless' and 'lazy', even though I had been dealt a hand that I didn't ask for. Exercise has been a huge part of my life for the past five years, and to be honest, I believe that it did save my life. I was on a very unhealthy and unsustainable path, weighing in at a mighty 18 stone (252 lbs) when I was 21. My diet pretty much consisted of pints of beer, cigarettes, and late-night takeaways; I'm not sure I even knew what a vegetable was unless it was deep-fried inside of a spring roll. I knew I had to change something to end the self-destructive mode I had allowed myself to slip into, so I 'attempted' to start running. This was a very long-winded process, starting with running on the treadmill until I had to stop, which was almost instantly. However, slowly but surely, I began to make some progress, and now I would go as far as saying that I love running and working out; the satisfaction post-workout is second to none. When I was first diagnosed, one of my biggest fears was having my exercise taken away from me, as the gym had now become a huge part of my life. It took me a while to adapt to this change, but I decided I was going to walk on my treadmill whenever I felt strong enough to do so. I truly believe that an hour of walking a day made a tremendous difference to my time during chemotherapy, it kept me strong, healthy, and determined. Now, at the time of writing this, just a month after finishing radiotherapy, I have signed up for my first-ever half marathon in less than two months' time. I'll say it was louder for the people at the back; **exercise saved my life.**

Food

Your body is going through so much during treatment; therefore, **food is your greatest friend.** There is a high chance that chemotherapy will bring a very unwanted guest into your life, known as nausea. It will run riot in your body at times, and eating will be the last thing on your mind as you focus on keeping other certain substances inside of you. I refer to these as the dark days and recommend regular small sips of ginger-infused water, and an abundance of sleeping through the pain. When you do have your better days, it is essential to refuel, replenish and give your body some well-needed TLC.

Forming a positive relationship with food will be incredibly beneficial to you. I am far from Gordon Ramsay myself and always swore by ready-cooked chicken, microwave rice and frozen veg as my main meals. Convenience was always the main focus. But getting into cooking was a key ingredient in my recovery process if you'll pardon the pun. I started off remarkably simple following the easiest recipes I could find, prioritising low-calorie and nutritious meals with plenty of vegetables and goodness.

A couple of recommendations that really helped kickstart my cooking habits would be trying out companies such as

HelloFresh and **Gousto.** These are meal kit retailers who provide you with a wide variety of meal options to choose from. They send you all the ingredients conveniently measured out for you with easy-to-follow recipe cards, making it ridiculously simple to cook delicious meals even for the most amateur chef. I'm not saying I do this every week, I certainly don't, as it can be on the pricier side. However, I really would encourage everybody to take advantage of the new customer sign-up offers, where the price is significantly discounted. By trying these services for even just one week, you will end up with five brand new meals that you can now reuse in the future as you have the recipe card, and you'll have a newfound confidence in cooking. Following the recipe cards that they provided helped me realise that it doesn't have to be difficult to cook delicious meals (not a sponsor). The 'Pinch of Nom' books are another stellar choice if you are in the market for some low-calorie delights, many of these recipes are now my regular meals throughout the week. Developing some sort of cooking skills has been an absolute game changer for me.

There is a brilliant book that I received as a Christmas present in the early days of my treatment, '**Anti-Cancer – A New Way of Life**' by Dr David Servan-Schreiber. The reason I mention this book here is because it also has a very extensive list of cancer 'superfoods', which helped me to stay healthy throughout chemotherapy. This was another tool I used to motivate myself with cooking, as I really wanted to get all these nutritious foods and ingredients into my diet, to give myself the best possible chance against this horrible disease. Here are some of the superfoods mentioned in the book: berries, dark chocolate, stone fruits, rosemary, parsley, oregano, soy, celery, broccoli, tomato, olives, olive oil, turmeric, green tea and plenty more! You will have to read the book to find out the rest of the information but trust me; you will not regret it.

Studying

I'm not going to sugar coat it for you, having cancer is miserable. Despite this, there is one advantage it gives us over the people still consumed by the busy hustle and bustle of the real world, which is extra time to work on ourselves. The biggest positive of my situation was the break from my hectic work schedule and life, this pause allowed me to reflect on my aspirations and envision my ideal future. I decided that if I was going to be taking a break from the world for a while, I would do my absolute best to use this time to my advantage. I wanted to be as productive as possible whenever I felt up for it to sculpt a better future.

I began looking for online courses to work towards. I have always been interested in the idea of coaching other people; the satisfaction of helping someone else achieve one of their goals fills me with joy. Having lost a substantial amount of weight myself, overcoming huge mental struggles and addictions along the way, I felt I had set myself up well to help others. At the start of last year, I decided to get my Level 2 Gym Instructing and Level 3 Personal Training qualifications. Unfortunately, due to unforeseen circumstances with my diagnosis shortly after passing these courses, I did not get the chance to use them. So, during treatment I looked for courses that linked closely to my goal of becoming a coach, with the aim of deepening my knowledge and positioning myself for success in the future.

I was recommended a website called **www.centreofexcellence.com,** which turned out to be my best friend for the next couple of months. It has a vast array of fully accredited courses to choose from, and if you search the 'discount codes' section on the page and use the code provided, the courses are much more affordable. There are certainly more in-depth and challenging courses out there, but if you are looking for something that isn't going to consume your entire life, while still delivering some fantastic information, then these courses could be for you. I wasn't looking to start a full degree at this point because, let's face it, cancer was still firmly dictating my life and I had to work around that. So, for me the flexibility and intensity of these courses were perfect. They are split into different sections with a test of your knowledge at the end of each. I completed a life coaching course, followed by a CBT (cognitive behavioural therapy) course, and now I am looking to start a nutrition course to add to my personal training portfolio; you will never regret improving yourself. It is imperative that you continue the fight, even in the bleakest of times.

Journalling

If I had a penny for every time somebody suggested journalling to help with anxiety, I would be an extremely rich man. If I had a penny for every time I took them up on that advice, then there wouldn't be many funds in the bank of George. That is until I started treatment. In the initial stages of my diagnosis, the overwhelming number of thoughts racing through my mind was crippling. I did not know where to begin, what questions to ask, or how to just give myself a few minutes of peace, without having to battle the onslaught of worries that were consuming me whole. I was never the type of person to journal my thoughts. To be honest, I always saw it as a waste of time and opted for what I believed was a far more superior approach: burying my thoughts deep down like they never existed (sounds healthy, George).

One night, I remember lying in bed feeling as if the pressure of my thoughts was going to make me explode. I reached for the closest piece of paper that I could find, which was an envelope, and began frantically scribbling down every single thought that was preventing my mind from resting, as if I had been possessed. That night was the most incredible sleep I had in weeks, I felt instant peace, and the very next day I went out and bought myself a journal.

Of course, the worries still exist in my life, but I am completely converted to journalling as a self-help tool. It prevents you from desperately clinging on to every single thought inside of your head and allows you to release some of your emotions onto the page, like a mini therapy session. We constantly put pressure on ourselves in our minds, which builds up over time without even being aware of it. Sometimes, writing it down can feel like the pin to pop the balloon, our problems often seem less scary after jotting them down. Give it a try before you go to sleep at night. Write down your thoughts, feelings, and just how your day went in general and see how it can free up your mind, even for a little moment of peace. A journal can also be a valuable tool to look back on in the future. You can see what made you feel happy on certain days, and what challenges you have overcome. It also provides you with the opportunity to remind yourself of just how strong you are. You are a warrior.

Plan For The Future

I think I can speak for most of us when I say we are not exactly where we want to be in life. Many of us get sucked into a routine and tend to just follow the path that gets laid out in front of us. Before we know it, we are working a job that we don't particularly like with very little time to do the things we enjoy. The fast pace of everyday life really can take hold of you, and when you do get some free time, you usually feel too tired to do anything productive with it. You just want to chill out and allow your mind to rest for a moment, and I can completely relate.

All my life, I have taken the straightforward way out. Risks made me uncomfortable, so I avoided them and stayed in my little bubble, only interacting with people when obliged. I have always just allowed my life to unfold around me naturally, living on autopilot, floating through my reality, barely aware that I could have any control over my destiny. It was only when the cold reality of having cancer kicked in, and the realisation of how short life can be devoured my every thought, that I started to question everything I have done with my life up until this point. "Was this really the future I desired?" I would ask myself. I was determined to use this time to create a better future, one where I could do something I enjoy, while having the freedom to soak up all of life's other luxuries, such as travelling the world. This shift in mindset was quite possibly the most crucial turning point in my life. It opened the possibility of change for myself, a glimmer of hope. I began planning for my future, and I started thinking about what I wanted to do with my life. This is when I decided to start looking into coaching as I knew I would love to help other people, and that is the reason I am writing these words today.

This incredibly difficult period of your life can seem very uncertain, but thinking ahead will give you the hope and strength that you need. It will keep your mind occupied and focused on the little glimmers of light at the end of the tunnel, making you more determined than ever. Research careers, plan holidays, create your five-year plan, keep looking forward and never give up. Everybody's situation is entirely unique during treatment for different cancers, which I completely understand. However, I believe keeping that faith and looking forward will positively impact your days during chemotherapy, and your outlook on life. Always keep fighting, you deserve it.

Learn A New Skill

Now, this recommendation was very much trial and error for me. I toyed with a few new 'skills' during my time, but I still stand by it. Every single one of us has at least one thing that we would love to try but just never feel as though we have the time for it. Well, I hate to sound like a broken record, but now we just might have the time for it.

Before fixating on the coaching route, I was determined that I wasn't going to return to a warehouse after treatment. So, I started trying my hand at a Microsoft Excel course to touch up on my computer skills and, at the bare minimum, land myself an office job. I soon realised that it wasn't for me, but it was a new skill I had attempted during my time off. My next big dream was learning to play the guitar (I can now play three chords). I tried drawing, yoga, and baking, it's fair to say that I did not master any of them, but I enjoyed myself and kept my brain occupied. You do not need to come out of treatment as the next prodigy of your chosen skill, but keeping yourself busy and, once again, adding another string to your bow during your time off is extremely beneficial. Your new talent could also provide you with a fantastic opportunity to connect with others along the way, a huge boost for your confidence and self-esteem which are both prone to taking a hit right now. Like I've said before, the days can be long and miserable if you let them; it's all about finding ways to keep yourself out of those dark places. This is a mental battle you must win.

Keep A Good Routine

Although it may sound simplistic, keeping a healthy routine is fundamental for all of us to fulfil our potential. Getting a bit off track is incredibly easy, and believe me, it's even easier to lose your way during treatment when your whole life feels like a simulation. A regular plan during chemotherapy is a totally foreign concept. Everything you know will have changed immensely, so it is vital that you create a solid structure for yourself and master the basics.

Chemotherapy is a harsh treatment, so your body is going through a lot; that is why you need to be kind to yourself now more than ever. Drink plenty of water to keep yourself hydrated and infuse it with some ginger to help with the nausea. Get out of the house when you feel up for it but remember to be sensible. Your immune system is very weak at this time; therefore, it is significantly easier to pick up illnesses which can prevent your treatment from progressing, slowing you down from returning to your normal life. Take yourself out on a walk or see friends for a coffee, but just always be mindful of the fact that you are more prone to illness and infection at this current moment. I highly recommend getting yourself some vitamins to take daily. I know money can be tight, but if you can invest in some multivitamins and turmeric tablets to reduce inflammation, then you're already ahead of the game. The impact of cancer goes a long way past a couple of tablets, but doing the bare minimum to nourish your body and give yourself the best chance possible is the key. Don't roll over and take it, fight back!

Fatigue will be a big part of your life; it will kick in sporadically throughout the day. You must listen to your body and rest when needed, meaning you may have to adopt the habit of napping in the middle of the day. The increased likelihood of an afternoon nap, combined with all the other chaos in your body right now, will make it more difficult to keep to a good sleeping schedule at night, but try your best to keep to a regular bedtime where possible. It became very tempting to stay up late in the early days of treatment, and I would suddenly become inspired to change my entire life at night. The fact that I usually didn't have any reason to get up early meant I began slipping into that unhealthy habit of staying up late. I would be hopelessly scrolling through my phone, creating even more anxiety within myself and achieving absolutely nothing by doing so. Once I managed to get myself back into my regular sleeping pattern, using various relaxation methods listed in this book, I felt miraculously more energised. I was able to achieve more with my day and felt more in sync with the people around me, which brings me conveniently to my next point.

Do Not Shut Off From The People Around You

Keep communicating with your friends, family and loved ones. As tempting as it may be, do not close yourself off from the people who want to be there for you. **You are not a burden!** For as long as I can remember, conveying my feelings has been a real challenge, and I am still no expert. I always found it difficult to express how I was feeling to the people closest to me, as I didn't want to cause them any worry. I didn't want sympathy, and I thought I could just bottle it all up and deal with it myself. Having that time to reflect on my life, I realised that dealing with problems in this way has in fact stunted my progression as a person. It has caused misery for myself and the people around me. I always believed by holding onto my problems, I was saving everyone else from the stress, and this only increased when I was first diagnosed. I struggled to talk to anybody about it because I believed that I was a burden to my family if I expressed any sort of discomfort or unhappiness. Cancer will make you feel vulnerable, and it is incredibly easy to convince yourself that you are an inconvenience. If you can get yourself out of this mindset and start expressing your feelings to your loved ones, then you will realise how much easier the journey can be, they will appreciate it more than you will ever understand. Just think about it: if the roles were reversed, wouldn't you want to be there for your loved one as much as you could? **You are not a burden.**

It became so much easier the more I started to communicate, and I found a place to unload my frustration and feelings. I started posting on TikTok, where I met lots of wonderful people who would listen to how I was feeling and just talk to me during a very lonely time. If you told me a few years ago that I was now posting online, I would've laughed in your face, it would've been my absolute worst nightmare. Honestly, it turned out to be one of the best things I ever did. It gave me a place to vent, kept me motivated and eager to share what I had achieved with my day, and it taught me the importance of opening up and communicating my feelings. I feel closer to my family than ever, and I know they are grateful for me letting them know how I really feel when I need to. I'm still not perfect at it, but I'm improving every day, and it feels amazing. A great suggestion from my sister was to schedule a short conversation with your family, maybe once a week, where they can ask any questions they may have for you. It may sound silly, but it can be difficult for people to know when the right time is to ask you a question, and whether some topics may be a bad trigger for you in certain moments. This is a great opportunity for you all to get things off your chest, avoid any frustration, and prevent loved ones from treading on eggshells due to the delicate nature of this time. Everybody now knows where they stand, and the rest of the week can run smoothly with nobody feeling left in the dark. Remember, this is an incredibly challenging time for them also.

Books And Podcasts

Prior to my diagnosis, the last book I can recall reading voluntarily was 'The Twits' by Roald Dahl back in primary school. For some reason, no matter how hard I tried (which probably wasn't very hard at all), I could never seem to get into any book I started. People would often tell me about fantastic books that they couldn't put down, and I honestly could not relate to this at all. To me it was just a more tedious version of television, without all the enticing colours and visuals to distract my very simple mind. It wasn't until I received a book I mentioned earlier as a Christmas gift, 'Anti-Cancer: A New Way of Life' written by Dr David Servan-Schreiber, that it finally clicked for me. Now that I had a relevant book to read, given the fact that I had been served up my delicious diagnosis, I decided to give the whole reading thing another shot. This book completely changed my outlook on reading. I finally related to what people had been telling me about being unable to put a book down, on my first night of reading it, I found myself 80 pages in at 1 am. I would recommend this book to anybody on their cancer journey. It was enlightening, filled to the brim with useful information on how to look after yourself, and incredible heartfelt stories of others going through their heroic battles.

Once I reached the end of this book I was completely hooked, the sense of achievement from finishing it filled me with joy and I was now ready to put my newfound knowledge to the test.

Eager to start my next book, I dived straight into the remarkable Ross Edgley's 'The Art of Resilience'. If you haven't come across this man yet, then I highly encourage you to research him, the first man to swim around Great Britain along with countless other outrageous achievements. My admiration for this man is endless; after completing his book my motivation was through the roof, and that is why you MUST read it during this period of your life.

I completed seven books during treatment, which, for someone like me who has barely read seven books in my entire life, is groundbreaking stuff. I really believe self-improvement is crucial when you're going through a tough time. Use this time to better yourself, increase your knowledge, raise your ambitions, and return to the world with a vengeance to claim the future that you want. Once again, we are all in different situations, so I completely understand that not everything I say will relate to everybody. Nevertheless, if I can give you even a little bit of guidance and hope throughout your time, then I have done my job effectively. Do not underestimate the power of a resilient mindset, continue to look to the future and fight it to your full ability.

The use of podcasts became just as important for me, switching some of my television time for an educational or motivational podcast worked wonders. On days when motivation was low, I would listen to a Tony Robbins podcast or The Diary Of A CEO, immediately feel energised, and be walking on the treadmill within half an hour. There is so much out there for you to learn. Find a topic you are interested in and experiment with a few podcasts within that field, you will soon get a feel for what you like and who resonates with you. I was seeking fulfilment most of the time; I wanted to feel worthy, as it was very easy to feel useless when I couldn't do much. Anything that was improving me physically or mentally, no matter how big or small, was incredibly stimulating.

Manifestation

One of the many books I completed during treatment was 'Manifestation: 7 Steps to Living Your Best Life' written by Roxie Nafousi, a read that I thoroughly enjoyed. Now, this is another one that took a while for me to warm up to. To be honest, without the whole cancer fiasco I probably never would've given it a chance, but at a time like this, what did I have to lose? If you're not familiar with manifestation, in the simplest of terms, it is basically the idea that you can visualise the things you want in your life into existence. Manifesting is all about changing your mindset and the energy you are giving off to the universe. So, if you can start to think, believe, and act like something is going to happen to you, it eventually will.

An example of manifestation would be your dream career or relationship. If you can picture yourself landing the perfect job and believe it with all your energy, it will eventually happen. It is not meant to be some kind of witchcraft where everything you wish for comes true instantly, it takes lots of time and patience. You must be very specific with your visualisation and sincerely believe that it is going to come into your life. Roxie Nafousi splits the book into seven steps:

- Be clear in your vision.
- Remove fear and doubt.
- Align your behaviour.
- Overcome tests from the universe.
- Embrace gratitude without caveats.
- Turn envy into inspiration.
- Trust in the universe.

I don't believe manifestation will be for everybody, and I completely understand the scepticism from many, it is something I am still working on and trying to gain control over. However, it is now a part of my daily routine, and I wouldn't have it any other way. To me, it has become a very powerful tool for those moments where I need a quick change in mindset, to stop my thoughts from spiralling. We are all human, and of course we are going to have negative thoughts. But practising manifestation has helped me limit those pessimistic beliefs, contributing to my staggeringly more positive outlook on life.

This is the perfect opportunity to try new things that will shed some light on these desolate times. Remember, your mental health is just as crucial as your physical health. If you can get into the routine of visualising all the wonderful things you want to come into your life, and begin to believe that they will, then you will live a happier and more fulfilled life. Manifestation for myself is currently all about my career; every day I am focussing on what I want to do with my life and where I want to be. By writing this book, I am telling the universe that I want to coach people, and I believe wholeheartedly that I can do it, starting with this piece of work. Even if you don't fully believe that the universe will reward your positive energy in abundance, just by visualising what you want, give it a try. I think you'll find that the least it will do is encourage you to work on building a stronger mindset, allowing you to stay hopeful in a period of your life that can sometimes seem hopeless.

Be Kind To Yourself

All these recommendations can be fantastic ways to spend your time during treatment. However, it is very important that you **do not put pressure on yourself.** It became abundantly clear to me that my time through treatment was going to be very much up and down, the realisation that I needed to listen to my body and rest on those down days was a bitter pill to swallow. As I mentioned before, the last few years of my life have revolved heavily around my 44kg weight loss. I was a big boy, and since then I have adopted an active lifestyle. Having my PICC line fitted and being told that I should only partake in low-impact exercise such as walking, felt like a huge segment of my life had been stripped from me. At this point, exercise had become 90% of my personality. For a while, this did hurt me. The thought of potentially having all my hard work ruined shook me to my core; anxiety ran riot throughout my body. It took some time to adapt to this new lifestyle, but I had already decided that I was going do all I could to return to full health as soon as possible. Rest became a crucial part of my recovery; it turned out to be a blessing in disguise for me. It helped speed up the process as I was allowing my body to heal, and I also believe it encouraged me to focus on my nutrition more because I was conscious about gaining weight. Your body will tell you when to rest, so make sure you listen and allow yourself to enjoy your home comforts in these times, without feeling guilty.

Cartoons are something that have always brought me comfort, so binge-watching Bob's Burgers in bed became a staple in my new routine. If you're a gamer, then use this time to play those games that you feel you usually don't have time to enjoy. I found comedy podcasts were another light-hearted way to wind down. I spent many hours listening to 'The Basement Yard' and 'Picky Boys' podcast, laughing away my troubles at the most ridiculous topics, but it just felt good to take the pressure off and allow myself to relax guilt-free. I often found that if I just allowed myself to rest when needed, then a more energised day would come along before I knew it. Really try to focus on the little victories and break your journey down into small steps to avoid overwhelming yourself. It becomes a one-day-at-a-time approach. I would tell myself to just make one small step towards my goal every single day, this could be as simple as making a healthy meal, going for a walk, or doing ten minutes of meditation. As long as I felt that one of my actions was a small contribution to bettering myself, I was satisfied.

Embrace The Change In Mindset

One thing that my nurses repeatedly told me was cancer would drastically change my mindset. Such a radical experience becomes a very severe eye-opener, and your outlook on the world around you will be completely different. Welcome this change with open arms. Once you realise that life is incredibly precious and can be taken away from you so easily, you will develop a much deeper appreciation for the little things in life, realising the situation is often not as bad as you first thought.

I was ridiculously guilty of over-catastrophising any minor inconvenience in my life, just like a lot of people in this world. We like to complain and pretend that bad things always happen to us. We tell ourselves that we can never catch a break because it makes us feel better. We often create these beliefs because it gives us an excuse to try less or give up; we stay in our comfort zone and carry on playing the victim because it's the easy route out. This perspective did change significantly for me after my diagnosis; I became remarkably more grateful for the position I was in. I felt frustrated that I had wasted so much of my life being miserable and depressed about situations that did not matter a great deal. You may even begin to feel differently about certain people in your life and their beliefs. Things that they complain about, which you used to understand, may now begin to irritate you as you see them as unnecessary negativity, and that is 100% okay. Don't allow yourself to feel any guilt for these changes or convince yourself that you're a bad person, because you're not. You have just been through a very traumatic period of your life, and it has blessed you with a new, enlightened approach to creating a better future for yourself. Enjoy your new appreciation for life and use it as motivation to get to where you want to be. If it means moving on from certain people, completely changing career paths, or setting off to travel the world, then absolutely go for it. For me, the change in mindset has allowed me to write this book, to try and create a future for myself where I can follow my passion for writing, helping others and making the most of the one opportunity I have on this planet!

Step Out Of Your Comfort Zone

By this point, I'm sure it will not come as a surprise to you when I tell you that I am an anxious person. It is something I have lived with for many years, and I make it my mission to keep it at bay. One of the most frustrating parts of anxiety, is that confronting the things that make you anxious is often the best way to overcome the problem, a truly vicious cycle. This phase of your life will more than likely involve more time in solitude than usual. Being away from your working environment and having many aspects of your social life on hold while you allow your body to recover, can very easily translate into feelings of sadness and anxiety. Think back to the coronavirus pandemic, I'm sure many of you will have suffered more with your mental health during this time, or at least know somebody who struggled to come to terms with their new isolated reality. It is fundamental that you don't allow yourself to slip too deep into your comfort zone while spending more time at home.

I can only speak for myself, but I found it very easy to start putting things off in my life and build up feelings of anxiety over very simple scenarios. When I say step out of your comfort zone, I mean it in very simple terms; for example, I began to start worrying about answering phone calls and messages. I often found it difficult to speak on the phone, and when I found myself feeling worried and stressed, I had a bad habit of shutting off and not wanting to communicate. So, stepping out of my comfort zone at that time was as simple as making sure I was answering the phone when it rang, or being the one to call my nurse when I had any questions, instead of getting my mum to do it for me (yes at the ripe old age of 25 I was running to my mum for help). I also found I began to build up pressure on myself about simple trips out of the house, so I made sure every week I was going out and doing my food shopping. Just very simple steps to prevent anxiety from taking over me. If you do begin to experience these feelings, then try to take a small step every day towards confronting them: reply to that message that you've been putting off, do your weekly shop, meet up with your friend, or even post on your social media account to get some of the tension off your chest. It will help you control your mental state and keep you in the right frame of mind to return to reality when the time is right.

Schedule Worry Time

This technique is changing my life; it is the practice of gifting yourself an allocated amount of time during the day, where you can focus on the things you are worried about. If you are anything like me, inconvenient thoughts race uncontrollably through your mind every single day; this can be very overwhelming and, quite frankly, a pain in the backside. So, I want you to start giving yourself a set time of the day, where you're allowed 15-30 minutes to direct all your focus and energy towards problems that are concerning you. I like to schedule mine before bedtime as I find it incredibly relieving to release all the tension and stress, allowing for a better night's sleep. During this time, I want you to let loose and embrace unloading all your worries into some sort of journal, making sure you get everything out. I guarantee you will already feel a huge sense of relief from this simple task, like scratching an itch that you were struggling to reach.

The next part of the process is to try and write down what small steps you can take towards resolving this issue. It doesn't have to be groundbreaking; it's just the very first step that will put you on the path to conquering this worry. For example, as a previously plump individual, my worries often revolve around my weight. So, my first step may be to prepare myself a nutritious lunch the night before, to eliminate the temptation of grabbing something easy and potentially significantly higher in calories. If your worries are about your career, the first step could be to create an account on a job searching website, and for financial worries it could be to put £5 into a savings account this week. These small steps are not going to rectify your problems instantly, but they get the ball rolling, and if you stick to these rules, then they will slowly become habits.

Finally, set yourself a reminder to check back on your progress at a certain time; once you feel you have accomplished this, then you can add your next small step to keep working towards eliminating this worry for good. This is such a powerful tool because you are giving yourself permission to worry at a specific time of day. Once your brain knows that it will be allowed this time later, you will find that the constant cycles of concern throughout the day will decrease remarkably.

The 10-Minute Rule

This one goes out to all my fellow procrastinators; I feel your pain. If you're prone to putting off tasks that you know need doing, give this method a try. We all know that starting something is the hardest part and often puts us off altogether. I found this was even more common for me during treatment due to all the other heightened emotions I was experiencing. The ten-minute rule is where you tell yourself that you are going to start a task for just ten minutes, set yourself a timer, and when it goes off you are allowed to stop that task. Again, giving yourself permission to stop after the time limit has been reached is a very powerful technique, and once you have reached the ten-minute mark, you will often find that you want to carry on with the task you have started.

The idea is to take the pressure off, preventing you from feeling overwhelmed by breaking it down into manageable sections. Once you have overcome the mental barrier of starting something, you will more than likely get into a rhythm as you realise that it wasn't as daunting as first anticipated. If you're still not fully convinced after the ten minutes, set yourself another timer and try again. Always allow yourself the option of stopping to prevent the build-up of unnecessary pressure.

For me, I found it essential to keep myself motivated and productive whenever I could. I was already battling all the emotions of a cancer diagnosis and the miserable side effects of chemo; therefore, using this method to achieve even ten minutes of productivity out of each day worked wonders. It helped me write many of the words you are reading right now, even on the days when I wanted to the least. Ten minutes out of your day to do a task is nothing, but what it can lead to could change your entire life. So next time you find yourself procrastinating, set yourself a timer and see how you get on. Because usually we have built it up in our heads into something much greater than it is. Once you have simplified it and removed the long commitment, you will probably end up enjoying the task and find tremendous satisfaction in completing it. Apply this approach to work, reading a book, exercising, or whatever you enjoy doing, and if you get to the end of your time and still don't want to continue, then that's fine; allow yourself the break and try again at another time.

Meditation, Gratitude, Positive Affirmations And Mantras

I'm not going into too much detail here, mainly because I am no expert. However, these are topics that greatly interest me and areas I am striving to improve in. My journey began more with positive affirmations; standing in front of the mirror and telling myself how great I am felt unnatural to say the least. In fact, the thought of complimenting myself in the slightest has always made my stomach churn. My newly adopted positive outlook on life, from the small inconvenience of cancer reminding me that life's too short, gave me the kick up the backside I needed to give the affirmations a go. I wish I was lying to you when I tell you that I started with a technique I like to call, 'partial affirmations'. By this, I mean I looked at myself in the mirror and said things like 'You're not as bad as you used to be, I suppose,' or 'Your loose skin doesn't look too prominent today.' For some reason, this felt more palatable for me; it eased me in gently until I was able to start giving myself a little more credit. This soon built up, the ridiculousness began to wear off and I felt less silly talking to myself in the mirror. As I grew more confident, I even started throwing in some Tony Robbins power poses, using my body and voice to emphasise the phrases I was using. He explains the benefits of standing in strong poses, for example, hands on your hips like superman, and really using your voice to convey confidence in your own ability. You must really believe in what you are saying. This is now a part of my daily routine. Yes, some mornings I wake up for work at 5:30 am and think, there is absolutely no way I will believe a word I say to myself right now, and on those days my affirmations may be left until later in the day. Sometimes, I will say them before I go to the gym or even just before I go to sleep, but now they are non-negotiable, they get done no questions asked. These are of a much kinder nature now, 'I am improving every day,' or 'Your loose skin is a reminder of how far you have come.' Now, to really confuse you (and myself), I'm beginning to throw some Mantras into my daily practice. Again, this is all new territory to me as well, but mantras are more of a short, powerful statement that you repeat multiple times. I seem to have latched on to "I will win because I will not stop." It's cheesy, I know, but I'm determined to get to where I want in life. At the end of the day, we live on a floating rock, so do what makes you happy.

Let's get into the big one now: meditation, a daunting concept for many of us. I'm still very much in the early stages of meditation, and I want this book to be completely real and authentic, so I will only be speaking on my limited knowledge. I started out following 5–10-minute guided meditations on YouTube. Every time I felt my mind wandering, I would refocus and try to really appreciate the silence and tranquillity of the moment. At first, I found my mind was always thinking about 100 different things, but I persevered with it, focusing on my breathing and heartbeat to re-centre my focus. I can now proudly announce that I am enjoying a solid 15 minutes of unguided meditation, just me and my thoughts taking a well-needed break from the world. I like to implement some gratitude into my meditation by reflecting on 3 things that I am grateful for in my life. Some days, these are very specific things that have recently occurred. Whereas other days, I may just be thankful for waking up in the morning or having my parents in my life. This has played a crucial role in my self-development journey of appreciating what I have. I am working very hard on not comparing myself to others as much; comparison is the thief of joy, so just appreciate what is yours.

ASMR

If you're not familiar with the concept of ASMR, just think: have you ever come across somebody whispering to you or tapping various objects on social media? If you haven't, then you are missing out. If you've made it this far, then you'll know that I'm on a mission to break down those barriers of scepticism that most of us have. Please trust me on this one and give it a try. ASMR stands for 'autonomous sensory meridian response', which is basically the little tingly sensation you feel travelling down your spine from certain sounds.

This is something I began using way before my cancer diagnosis, but it rescued me from some frightful sleepless nights during chemotherapy. Once you allow yourself past the original awkwardness of ASMR and just embrace its slightly obscure nature, then I'm almost certain you'll be in a state of complete zen by the end of it. It will take some time to adapt; you need to have a look around, find which artists you like, and determine what style of video is going to get you tingling. There are plenty of sound triggers out there: tapping, scratching, whispering, and a vast array of others. The purpose of these videos is to quite simply make you tingle and ultimately feel relaxed. You will find that there is a central theme in many of the videos, to try and help you sleep, which I can confirm you will be seeking answers to this problem rather frequently during treatment. With the many unpleasant side effects of chemo such as my nemesis nausea, you will need a good old reliable method of relaxation, the ultimate distraction and stress reliever. I believe ASMR was exactly that for me during some of my toughest nights. I started off simple with some tapping and calming sounds to help me unwind. But I am man enough to admit that I have since delved deep into the world of role-playing videos, and you will not get an ounce of shame out of me for it. I have relaxed in fantasy taverns, had hot chocolate whipped up for me in a cosy café, been on spa days, and flown first class on a luxurious airline, all in the fictional world of ASMR (and I would do it all again). go into it with an open mind, find what works for you, and feel your worries gently drift away for a while. At the very beginning of my treatment, I was very unwell from receiving my COVID jab that I had naively neglected getting before starting chemo. I don't think I'm being too dramatic when I say I owe my life to ASMR and hot water bottles for that week. Well maybe a little dramatic but you get my point. That also reminds me, get a hot water bottle, the superior tried and tested method for any aches and pains.

The Relaxation Bundle

You are in for a treat now, ladies and gentlemen. This one is a concoction of a few coaching/relaxation methods that, I believe, come together to create the perfect package of tranquillity. Basically, it's an amalgamation of a few elements from my various courses that I found of interest, put into their simplest forms by myself, of course. Let's set the scene; I like to spend a bit of time on this one, with minimal lighting to distract me, candles lit, wax melt on for some calming aroma, and preferably laid down on my bed. Whatever ultimate relaxation looks like to you, that's what you're striving for. Now, the first technique we are introducing is **abdominal breathing,** which is essentially deep breathing (groundbreaking stuff, George, I know). For me, getting my breathing under control first instantly makes me feel more relaxed. Place one hand on your chest, one hand on your stomach, and breathe in through your nose filling your lungs with as much air as possible. Notice how the hand on your stomach rises while the hand on your chest stays still. Hold this for a couple of seconds, and then release it, allowing your stomach to sink back to its regular position as the air escapes. Focus on each breath you take from start to finish, and begin to let go of the thoughts that are troubling you. You'll have plenty of time to dwell on these during your scheduled worry time later. Repeat this process until you feel a shift in the pattern of your thoughts. When you are consciously thinking about the oxygen passing through your body, and the feeling of your heart beating steadily in your chest, you know you are heading in the right direction. The timings can vary depending on the mental state you are in when beginning the process. I usually find 10-15 of these breaths works for me, to which I then slowly transition into a nice steady breathing rate, ensuring I still pay attention to every inhale and exhale.

Now that you have your breathing right where you want it, it's time to get the body up to speed, and this is where **body scanning** enters the chat. Part two is very simple as no physical action is necessary. Lie as motionless as you can, but begin to think about any areas of your body that are holding stress or tension. Start from your feet and work upwards, really try to connect with yourself, and identify the problem areas that have built up. Yes, I'm cringing at myself writing this part, but you really do need to try and feel everything. I do not want you to act on anything yet. Just take a few minutes to scan every inch of your physique, and make a mental note of the areas that you would like to kindly ask the pressure to F off. We all have certain zones where we hold on to stress, anxiety, worry and all those glorious things, so now that you've found yours, it's time to give it the boot.

Part three of the package is **progressive muscle relaxation**, an intriguing way of telling you to repeatedly tense your muscles (there's more to it than that, I promise). Now, go to work; start with the muscle you feel is your biggest issue, and squeeze it as tight as possible for a five-second hold. For example, if you're feeling tension in your arms, ball your fist up and grip tight. For your legs flex your foot, squeeze your glutes, or do whatever you need to do to tense the desired area. Notice how the muscle feels when fully contracted; that's all I want you to think about for those five seconds, and then release. Your focus is now primarily on the sensation of the muscle returning to its resting state. I want you to imagine that this is all the pent-up negative energy leaving your body; allow this to feel like a weight being lifted off your shoulders. Repeat this process a few times until your entire body feels less rigid. I usually spend 5-10 minutes on this part, and by the end of it I feel loosey-goosey baby.

Finally, we introduce the icing on the cake, **visualisation**. As always, there are copious amounts of detail that I could go into on this topic, but in Layman's terms, it is imagining yourself living your dream life in the present moment. You can use visualisation in different ways; however, I use it as a glorified daydream. I envision myself in the ideal scenario that I crave to be in at that exact moment. Many of these sessions are spent picturing myself strolling along a beach with a beer in hand. Recently, I have been imagining myself as a successful author and coach, helping others achieve their dreams while getting paid for it. This has helped to reduce my anxiety massively. When I feel myself getting a little bit run down, it allows me to escape to a place where I feel fulfilled and empowered. It reminds me of what could be waiting for me, and why it is crucial that I continue to work hard on myself. Honestly, this exercise is very time-dependent for me. If I'm still feeling good and have nowhere to be, I let it run until I'm back in whatever mindset I desire. I find that my mind tends to wander to other happy places, and maybe begins to visualise the specific steps of getting to that place. Just enjoy the process and welcome the outcome it brings.

Learn To Live In The Moment

Something you're almost certain to do when you receive your cancer sentence is think your entire life is over, and everything is worthless. Please refrain from doing so. A valuable lesson we can all learn, particularly during our time with cancer, is how to be present today. Initially, my mind raced into the future thinking about how my life was basically over for the next few months. I constantly thought about when treatment would end, and what the point of my existence was. When I really thought about it, I realised that I had been doing this for pretty much my entire life. Always thinking ahead about how it probably wouldn't work out anyway, so what's the point? How many days of my life have I already wasted because of this toxic mindset? Where could I be in my life right now if I hadn't allowed myself to think like this? Now I knew how fragile and precious life really was, I was certainly not prepared to function like this any longer. What I have learned is that we must focus on the now. Whatever it is you want to do with your life, **take the first step and the next one will reveal itself**. If you look too far ahead and try to plan your life out from start to finish, you will be consumed by fear, worry, and self-doubt. The plan will change many times throughout the process anyway, so it's completely counterproductive to try and fully map it out. Whatever it is that you want to achieve, no matter how great or small, be here today. Have an idea and take that initial step; watch the second step of your journey unfold in front of your very eyes. Often, doing one thing will lead to a completely unexpected outcome, and that is how most people discover something they enjoy. I cannot explain to you how many times I have got myself in a state of total infuriation, because I've tried to sketch out my entire life in one sitting. It always ends in disappointment, so now I'm learning to go with the flow and embrace the uncertainty, that's where the greatest success comes from. So, start enjoying today and appreciating what you have right now. I just make my little TikTok's, write my book, spend time with the people I love, and I've never been happier.

A Fresh Start Filled With New Opportunities

Undergoing treatment can make you feel like you're losing progress in areas of your life that you've worked incredibly hard at. For me, this goes back to the gym again, shock. Not being able to work out was upsetting to begin with; all the progress I had made felt totally pointless, and I was feeling sorry for myself. For the first few weeks, I really struggled to come to terms with the void it left in my life. I spent large parts of my day watching fitness videos on YouTube; a YouTuber called Glen Gillen got me through some tough times. I couldn't stop thinking about how far I was falling behind everybody else who was still in the gym. The thought of all my biggest lifts decreasing shook me to my core. It sounds dramatic, but these are the kinds of thoughts that were occurring daily. I knew this wasn't sustainable, and I had to change this mindset for my own sanity. I thought long and hard about this; what if I could flip this into a positive? This could be a new challenge for me. Yes, I had to drop the weight significantly when I returned to the gym (along with my pride), but this meant I got the chance to hit the little personal records again. The way I see it, I now have a new opportunity to start fresh, perfecting things along the way and allowing myself to enjoy the journey. The world always seems to be moving at 100 miles per hour, and we're constantly rushing through most things we do just to keep up with everyone around us. What I have learnt from this new start is that when you do slow down and embrace the refresh, you'll probably notice that many things you do are not being done to the best of your ability, because you've streamlined them for the sake of time. With this newly adopted mindset, my training has never been better; I've stopped worrying about lifting the heaviest weights possible in the shortest amount of time. Now, I'm focussing on my technique, slow and controlled movements, and enjoying the steady improvement while I learn to **live in the moment.** I am very fortunate to be back doing what I love, so why not enjoy it instead of constantly comparing myself to others and wishing it all away? This can be applied to so many aspects of your life, whether it's your work or hobby. Don't let cancer take away what you've worked hard for; enjoy the new challenge and the feeling of smashing your goals all over again. You've got this.

Be Selfish And Do What Makes You Happy

I've always been guilty of being a chronic people-pleaser. I enjoy being liked, which isn't necessarily a bad thing, but I do believe that it has held me back to a certain extent. One of the toughest challenges I have faced so far is learning how to put myself first more often. I've always been petrified of how other people view me. I found myself apologising for things I hadn't done or agreeing to help others and ultimately overloading myself. The guilt of saying no to somebody could ruin my entire week. I'm telling you now that this does not work during treatment; you will not have the energy or capability to please everybody. You need to be focused on keeping yourself healthy and happy by any means necessary. This is your reminder that it doesn't make you a bad person if you say no to somebody. It just means that you're saying yes to your own needs instead.

Your time is incredibly precious so you MUST use it wisely. People will completely understand why you're putting yourself first given the situation you are in, and if they don't, then they're not worth pleasing anyway. Work on yourself when you can, do what YOU want to do, not what you think will make other people happy, and protect your inner peace at all costs.

When I first returned to work after treatment, I had one week at the end of August when I was feeling a bit down, so I started listening to Christmas music during my shift. Christmas is my favourite time of the year and fills me with instant joy. Life has taught me that it doesn't follow any rules by blessing me with cancer at the age of 25, so why should I follow them? If blasting Mariah Carey out in 25-degree heat is going to give me instant happiness, then that is exactly what I will do. Life has no rules, therefore, neither do I, and I will not apologise for it. People can think I'm a little bit strange or disagree with what I do, and that's okay because I'm embracing this newfound mindset, and it feels amazing. As for the guilt, you can't just turn it off like a switch, but I'm pushing through and learning to live with it because I now know how valuable my time is. As much as we care about others, we all have our own priorities at the forefront of our minds. Remember that everybody is looking out for themselves; do what is going to make YOU shine.

Pleasure And Mastery

Now, this one is a coaching technique that really helped shape my own personal daily routine. Pleasure and mastery is a cognitive behavioural therapy technique, first described by Aaron T Beck, that is used to help treat depression. You start by recording a weekly activity journal for yourself, listing all the activities that you participate in every day.

The easiest way to do this is by creating a table for every day, split into hourly sections, and then filling in the gaps with how you spend that hour. You want to include everything you can: brushing your teeth, going for a walk, taking a nap, it will all help. After a week of filling in your activity journal, I want you to go back over your activities and mark them with either a 'P' for pleasure or an 'M' for mastery. Pleasure refers to any activity that brings you joy, something that you do just to make yourself feel happy. Good examples of this would be watching a movie or playing a game.

On the other hand, mastery is all about activities that give you a sense of accomplishment such as: studying, learning a new skill, or completing a household task like doing your washing. The final part is to give each activity a rating out of 10. This is just a rough guide of how much pleasure or sense of accomplishment this task is providing you with. It was a game changer for me, because I realised how much my mastery tasks had slipped at that time. It became apparent just how much my dip in mood correlated with my lack of balance between pleasure and mastery activities, and that is exactly what you need in your life: a healthy balance of the two. 100% pleasure after a while can often lead to a feeling of unfulfillment, and you may start to feel miserable as you have no productivity in your life. I know that I am at my absolute worst when I'm feeling useless. Often, the tasks that I dread the most make me feel bulletproof when I finally tick them off my list. On the other hand, all mastery leads you to only one destination, and that is burnout. This is significantly more important during treatment: you are increasingly prone to burnout, so remember to **be kind to yourself.**

I had plenty of napping and watching comedies on my schedule, which was not a problem at all. However, with very few mastery activities on the cards, I was on a one-way train to depression town. As I slowly started to re-introduce some productivity and get my life back on track, I finally started to feel like myself again, completely rejuvenated by the restoration of balance in my schedule. I think this technique played a huge part in the structure of this book; most of what I have written about is essentially just a giant pleasure and mastery list. The aim for my days through treatment was to nail that healthy balance, to keep myself feeling motivated on the good days, but well-rested and joyful on the days that I needed a little bit of that pleasure. So, create your own list, work out where your lack of balance lies, and slowly start to tip the scales back to even day by day. Very slight changes will have a drastic impact.

Tough Times Make Funny Stories

I don't know about you, but it doesn't take much for me to feel embarrassed; my awkwardness in social situations has been unmeasurable at times. Having said that, going through cancer has thickened my skin without a shadow of a doubt. I learnt very quickly that I was going to find myself in many uncomfortable situations along the way. Things that could quite easily completely demoralise my sensitive little soul.

I was gifted a taster of this just to ease me in before treatment had even begun, with a cheeky little trip to the fertility clinic. Chemotherapy poses a risk of infertility; therefore, it is recommended that you freeze some sperm as a precaution. Never in a million years did I think I would be in the car with my mum on the way to a sperm bank, and yet here I was at 25 years old, in complete silence, utterly mortified. The memory of entering the reception and making the most horrendously awkward eye contact, with the same faces I knew I would be seeing on the way out, will be ingrained in my brain forever. In the waiting room, I was handed a small container, given the debrief of the process, and sent on my merry way into my own private masturbation chamber. A vivid picture of the room comes to mind: a small sink, a tired-looking sofa full of shame and sin, a bright yellow hazardous bin in the corner for any waste from your wrongdoings, and four blank walls with a Wi-Fi password displayed in the centre, expressing full judgement. So many thoughts were racing through my mind: how long is an acceptable amount of time to be in here, where should I position myself, am I being watched, but mainly just insurmountable levels of discomfort and embarrassment consuming my entirety. Okay, enough of the explicit details from the room of shame. After an excruciating amount of time I left my chamber, dropped my sample off at the deposit window, and headed back to the waiting room to finish filling out a question form. Now, the members of staff that I encountered here were all nothing but caring and professional; they deal with these situations daily. However, I could not help but feel slightly distressed communicating with this lovely lady, knowing she was fully aware that I had just ejaculated in the room next door only 5 minutes ago.

I would be lying if I said to you that I left there that day with my head held high. I crawled back into my mum's car, with my tail between my legs, and did not mutter a single word to her on the way home. Having said that, nothing builds character quite like a bit of good old-fashioned trauma, and I know I am a stronger man from that experience.

I think the one that may take first place in the humiliation awards for myself, would have to be my first stool sample. Just after my first chemotherapy treatment, I had to get my COVID jab, this turned out to be a huge mistake as I was violently ill for several days. Apparently, chemo and COVID do not make for a good mixture. Up until this point, I had been fortunate with illness; I never seemed to pick up anything too concerning. With the risk of sounding dramatic, on this occasion, I felt so unwell that I started to wonder whether the chemotherapy had poisoned me, and my time on this planet had come to an end. On December 23rd, I had to go into the emergency assessment bay to be checked over. Once again, the staff were an absolute credit to Northampton General Hospital. They made me feel so comfortable and thoroughly examined me to find the exact problem. As part of the check-up, I was requested to provide a stool sample by a lovely young nurse, who helped make me feel at home. My last few visits to the toilet prior to this had been somewhat of a liquid, so you can imagine my concern when I was handed a cardboard tray and pointed in the direction of the individual toilet, being used by the entire bay.

I was instructed to collect my sample in the tray, leave it on top of the bin, and then alert the nurse when I had done so for her to collect it. Immediate alarm bells were ringing in my already anxiety-ridden mind. The only saving grace was that my stool was at least half solid by this point, so the cardboard tray's structural integrity was intact. Completely against every instinct in my body, I placed the tray on the lid of the bin, covered with a piece of toilet paper, vacated the restroom, and gave the subtle 'I've just done a poo' nod to the nurse to signal that the package was ready for collection. I really wish I could remember the name of the nurse, but I think the sheer humiliation of this day has put a mental block on many of the small details. That and the fact that I was barely able to stand up for longer than 30 seconds. Anyway, the delightful nurse responded to the nod and headed towards the toilet. I was beginning to struggle to stay on my feet, so I began slowly stumbling back to my seat, feeling confident that my stool was no longer in any danger of being discovered by another innocent user of the toilet. Little did I know that my troubles were far from over, as on the way to the collection point the nurse was stopped by another patient with quite an urgent matter, which she absolutely had to deal with. I completely understood the situation; however, amid it all, another elderly gentleman decided to use the lavatory, which, unbeknownst to him, was still occupied by my poo in a tray. The man was already halfway across the room when I heard him ask another nurse whether this particular door was for the toilet. I felt so horrendous that I could barely keep my head up. But of course, I was still observing the entire room like a hawk, anxiously awaiting the nurse's interception of the package. It was now certainly a code red. Torn between trying to maintain some discretion and realising the impending doom of this poor man discovering what I had left in the room, I half-heartedly let out an 'Excuse me, sir, the nurse needs to go in there first,' which he had zero chance of hearing. You could cut the tension with a knife (more than what could be said for my liquid poo). The poor nurse had one last-ditch attempt to save my dignity by politely calling over to the gentleman, 'Excuse me, sir, I need to go in there first.' Unfortunately, he was slightly hard of hearing and didn't catch this one either. It was now or never for me; I used every bit of strength I had at that moment to push out of my chair and intervene. Luckily for me, the elderly gentleman was also using a walking stick, therefore, even as the hollow shell of a man that I was, I just managed to win the footrace and prevent a catastrophe. I now had to explain to a rather confused man that he couldn't use the facilities just yet, as I was waiting for my excrement dish to be disposed of. This time, opting to uncomfortably wait at the toilet door with the bewildered elderly gentleman for the nurse's arrival, I really did question whether I would recover from this traumatic experience. I felt like I belonged in a cardboard hospital tray myself. Shortly after returning to my seat of shame, I was escorted to another section of the hospital for a scan by the same nurse involved in the whole faeces fiasco. I buried my embarrassment deep down and scraped together some small talk for what felt like a never-ending corridor to our destination. For some reason, asking if she had any nice Christmas plans knowing that she had just handled my waste tray, didn't feel completely appropriate.

My struggles with body confidence had to be quickly brushed aside as I got used to undressing for numerous scans and procedures, all of which felt like the end of the world in that moment. There are many more incidents throughout the journey that catapulted me out of my comfort zone, but I think I'll leave it there for now. Of course, many details of these stories are blown out of proportion in my mind. But the reason I am telling you this is because next time you find yourself in a traumatic situation, remember that it will all be a hilarious anecdote for you to exaggerate to people in the future. Just another one of the many tests that you overcame to become the strong, resilient person you are today.

Mental Health

I know I said I would leave the rest of my previous mental struggles for another time, but as I sit here today on World Mental Health Day 2023, I cannot help but feel inspired to write a few words on the subject. Let's call it a bonus section for you lucky readers. Discussing mental health, especially for men, is still something that can be very challenging. Although we are moving in the right direction, there is still plenty of work to be done. It truly is a topic very close to my heart; for as long as I can remember, I've battled with my mental health. I never felt like I had a reason to feel the way I did growing up. I had an amazing group of friends and an incredible family who gave me everything I needed, and yet here I was, completely engulfed by sadness. This only added to the problem, as not only did I feel depressed and anxious every minute of the day, but I also felt a huge sense of guilt for feeling this way in the first place, as if it was completely unjustified. I now know how silly that was as I couldn't help how I felt, and I shouldn't have been ashamed of it. But at the time, I felt like an awful, ungrateful human being. I always hated my own appearance; I cannot remember a time when I wasn't conscious of the way I looked. Thinking back, it may have stemmed from being called 'big head' in year three by an older kid. I remember going home and asking my mum what big head meant as, at this point, I was a completely oblivious child, unaware of the fact that I had a massive 'meathead' that was going to cause me a few problems in the big bad world.

My personal insecurities always made me quite reserved. Throughout my teenage years, I often avoided social events due to the fear of a humiliating comment being made about my appearance. These fears held me back from many things in my life. When I think about it, I was too afraid to pursue any interests of mine; I even quit my football team at 15 because I felt I was too fat for the kit. I had played football all my life and absolutely adored the game. But after months of stretching out my football shirt before the game and wrapping my entire body in Sellotape to try and hold my jiggly bits in, I decided the pre-match nerves were becoming too unhealthy and hung my boots up for good. It was shortly after this time that things began to really spiral. Towards the end of secondary school, it was as if a switch flicked in my head, and these feelings began to intensify to an uncontrollable level. I began to feel an insufferable urge to shut down from everybody around me. At school, I would no longer want to even leave the classroom to socialise at break times, so I asked my form tutor if I could spend my breaks inside alone. I began to drift away from everybody in my life as the powerful claws of depression took a firm hold on me. I have lost touch with some very special friends over the years because of my own poisonous mind, completely self-inflicted, but I regret it dearly. This was the start of some bleak years. I would take my dogs out for a walk after school, find the sharpest rock in the field, and start trying to cut myself with it as a bit of self-punishment for being the way I was.

Self-harm is another taboo subject, but one that I would love to help eliminate the stigma around it. Rocks eventually turned to blades. I never had the intention of ending my own life with self-harming, it was more just a form of punishment and a way of releasing pain, as I watched blood cover my entire body from multiple slices to my own flesh. I know this sounds incredibly morbid, and when I speak about it now, I have no idea why or how I thought this was the right thing to do. But I really want to try and portray just how tainted my mind was at this point in my life. The scariest thing looking back is that I used to hope that I would get a disease like cancer, something that would put me out of my misery guilt-free. To this day, it still devastates me that my mind used to think like that.

This is when the drinking really began at sixth form. I would often turn up just to sign in; then, I would head straight to the local co-op for a bottle of vodka to drink in a field near my school. This became such a common occurrence that I had a favourite log I used to sit on to drink. My friend Joe would quite often have to come and rescue me from the log if he hadn't heard from me in a while. The morning before the interview for my first ever job, I remember being in the shower drinking out of a Lucozade bottle that I had filled with three different types of wine, just so I would be confident enough to attend the interview. I dropped out of sixth form and went full-time at my job; however, my drinking continued to spiral, and I ended up being signed off work for months with depression. I was passed around various counselling establishments; unfortunately, at the time none of them were able to help me, as they could barely get a sentence out of me. I couldn't even make eye contact with them.

While I was signed off, I did work extremely hard on my weight; I managed to lose a considerable amount of 'timber' through exercise. Unfortunately, the drinking was still at an all-time high, so I just opted for lower-calorie options and cut down on my eating to save extra calories for alcohol. The weight loss didn't last long this time around; I returned to work and soon realised that I was just as miserable as ever. I completely fell off any sort of exercise regime and started to put all the weight back on, it became very clear that I needed to leave my job. I was turning up to morning shifts already drunk, and within an hour of starting, sneaking back out of work to hunt down more booze. I could no longer function without it.

My next job was the biggest mistake of all; I began working behind the bar at my local working men's club. Needless to say, it was the last place a depressed, overweight alcoholic needed to be. I was now three stone heavier than my previous highest weight, thanks to a diet of alcohol, cigarettes and takeaways. I was on a path to certain death. I lost everything I had at this time; I gambled away thousands of pounds in savings from my first job. I stole any money I could find around the house to finance my gambling and boozing, and I even had to sell my car to pay back the money I owed to my parents (not that I could use it much as I was always intoxicated). I used to gamble because I believed that I only had two viable options: either become rich enough to escape my current reality or be dead very soon. I felt there was absolutely no way I could carry on like this for much longer. It terrifies me to look back at some of the situations I have found myself in. I've been found in a bush halfway down the canal, picked up after falling off my bike from being too drunk to ride it home, and taken home from town because a police officer found me passed out with one shoe on. I don't think it's dramatic to say that I'm lucky to still be alive, and all of this seemed to stem from a deep self-hatred of my own appearance and way of being.

The list of terrifying events about my past that I could write about is endless, and I hope that I can continue to tell my story in the future. However, right now, I just want you to know that whatever you are going through, you certainly are not alone, and it can absolutely get better. I wish more than anything that I could travel back in time to that helpless, lost soul and tell him that everything is going to be okay. In fact, I wish I could hand him this book to show him where he is today. I am proud of how far I have come. Beating multiple addictions, significant weight loss, and slowly but surely regaining control of my life. It is far from easy to fight against the depression, but it is worth it. I realise now that I used to allow myself to feel sad because it was the easy way out of everything. Believing that the world was against me and that no good would ever come to me, was just a way of staying in my comfort zone. It was the perfect excuse to evade any improvement, instead just accept my depressing fate, sitting alone in my room with only my animal crossing village residents, and copious amounts of alcohol to keep me company. One small step can lead to a giant change, the life you want isn't as far away as you think, but it's up to you to start working towards it. I'm still in the process of figuring out what I want to do in life; I didn't plan on being here past 25 so I never saw much point in creating a future. But now I'm ready to work tirelessly for my happy ending. I want you to remember that the way you're feeling isn't your fault, but unfortunately, you're the only one who can begin to make a difference.

Recognising the problem is always the first step, so say it out loud. Lean on your friends and family in your time of need and share your troubles. Focus on yourself and what makes you happy instead of letting others dictate how you feel and act. Going through cancer this year was incredibly challenging at times, but the crazy thing is that it wasn't the hardest year of my life. Thanks to all the positive changes I have made over the last few years, I was ready for the fight. I was able to reflect upon previous years and just how low I was. I knew that I had put way too much effort into getting to this point in my life, and that I was not going to let anything stop me. I hope that if you are struggling right now, you too will one day look back and see just how far you have come. Life can get better, please keep pushing through with me.

Life After Cancer

When you hear about people's journeys through cancer, you will often be told that the hardest part can be returning to the real world, after being given the all-clear. Living in your little bubble while undergoing treatment ends abruptly, you are thrown headfirst into the deep end, expected to slot back into reality and pick up where you left off. It can be a very confusing time in your life. Of course, it is complete joy and elation beating cancer, you're completely overwhelmed by the fact that this nightmare has finally reached its climax. However, you're now released back into a world that has continued to progress without you, and your mindset has most probably changed quite noticeably.

The day I received my final scan was one of the best days of my life. It also happened to be the same day that my mum and dad had decided to get married, after more than 30 years of being together. The wedding was the perfect distraction for me. It had kept me from worrying about whether my cancer had been eradicated, to the point where 15 minutes before the ceremony, I had forgotten all about it. Just as we arrived at the venue, I received a phone call from my doctor. I stepped outside to listen to the news, as the sobering severity of this phone call began to flood back into my mind. I had done it; the cancer was gone, and the horror show that I had been living in for the past year was officially over! As relieved as I was, I knew the wedding was due to start in a few minutes, and I was incredibly excited, so I composed myself and headed back in. It was a very small ceremony with just the immediate family present, who were all well aware that I would be receiving this news today. They were more impatient to find out the news than I was, so I decided to just quietly whisper to my sister and girlfriend that it was good news, and I would tell them more after Mum and Dad had tied the knot. Well, to say that I had underestimated the impact of this passing comment would be putting it very lightly. Tears began streaming from them both as I was immediately pulled into the most violent bear hug from my sister, which nearly winded me. It was only at that moment I realised the significance of that phone call, and what it meant to everybody around me. The whirlwind wedding day had me completely underestimating what I had just achieved.

I realised that I had made some big changes in my life. I didn't run from my cancer diagnosis or bury my head in the sand, I faced it head-on and did everything I could to beat it as efficiently as possible.

This one piece of news meant that my hard work had paid off, I was cancer-free, and for once in my life, I was sincerely proud of myself for trying to be a better person. The cat was, of course, out of the bag now at the wedding as I began sobbing with pride alongside the girls. I was then encouraged to break the news to my mum and dad, who, unbeknown to me, were also eagerly awaiting the big news. It ended up being the most incredible day that will live with me forever. We now have a wonderful photo collection of us all blubbering uncontrollably, which I have since proudly made into a scrapbook for my parents as a wedding present.

Unfortunately, this doesn't mean that it's been all bells and whistles since finishing treatment. There have been some huge mental barriers that I have had to tackle so far and continue to work on, and I know there will be plenty more to come. Going back to work has been challenging. Returning to a job where you didn't necessarily feel fulfilled in the first place, after such a life-altering experience as cancer is no easy task. Seeing how your colleagues have progressed ahead of you can be tough, or you may no longer be remotely interested in your job role. You now see the world completely differently after being reminded of how quickly it can all be taken away. Fatigue can also play a part; your body must readjust to the long working hours after the extended break in routine during your treatment. To be honest, just getting back into the swing of being around people again should not be overlooked either. For me, it has been all of the above. I feel left behind, unfulfilled, shattered, and totally useless. Now, in the past, I would've accepted this as my fate and slipped deeper into that dark pit of depression that I was once so familiar with. But I'm too strong mentally now with all the work I have put in on myself. I know I am worthy of better; therefore, I am actively seeking new opportunities for my future that can bring me actual satisfaction. Make sure your return to work is slow and steady; do not feel pressured into taking on too much too soon. I started with a phased return to work on reduced hours, which increased weekly. Jumping straight back in could be detrimental to your health, remember you are your number one priority now.

My mindset has completely flipped from a few years ago following the advice listed in this book, and I'm happier than I've ever been. I am just grateful for my life and the opportunities in front of me. Even on the days that I'm not enjoying, I will now try to help myself with my techniques. Instead of sitting in my pit of misery, I will take a few minutes for some meditation or stick on a funny podcast. I am currently working my way through 'Chatabix' and 'Wolf and Owl'. Both podcasts consist of two comedians, filled with self-deprecation and comedy gold, they are brilliant. My intention is not to downplay the post-cancer period, it is an extremely challenging time of the process. But the more you battle it, the easier it gets, I promise you.

My most difficult days are always the ones that I make no effort to improve. However, these days are inevitable and totally acceptable. I have benefitted greatly from always making sure I have something planned, to either work towards or look forward to. My first goal after treatment was to get myself back in the gym to build my strength and fitness. As I allowed myself to **enjoy the process**, it felt unbelievable to see them both begin to improve again, and surprisingly quickly too. Within a couple of weeks of getting back to training, I had set myself my first big task. I signed up for a half marathon in London just three months after treatment. I now had the perfect reason to stick to a training plan and a healthy diet, which was still vital for my recovery. I cannot recommend taking part in an event like this enough; the feeling of crossing that finish line is indescribable. I managed to beat my 2-hour target as well with a time of 01:55:06, which was a great little bonus!

I've also enjoyed plenty of social events with my loved ones in the past few weeks: Oktoberfest, weekends away, interactive-games bars, bowling, and my first post-cancer holiday to Turkey, which will now be one of the most memorable holidays of my life. Ten days filled with sunshine, food and beer were exactly what I needed after this year.

Start setting yourself some challenging targets, even if they seem optimistic, because you are capable of so much more than you think. Training for my half marathon I felt like I was completely out of my depth, but I did it anyway, and now I'm pushing myself towards goals that I feel like I have no right aiming for. I am embracing the imposter syndrome and going for it anyway, fake it 'til you make it baby. Life will only improve if you try to make it better, and I know you have what it takes.

Farewell (For Now)

Ladies and gentlemen, unfortunately, we have reached the end of my timeless wisdom for now. I am somewhat of a serial waffler, but I promise you I did everything I could to keep this as precise and compact as possible. I feel incredibly passionate about the link between cancer and mental health; life is more than enough without a serious illness to contend with. Therefore, you need to be battle-ready to go toe to toe with cancer. I am now fully invested in the future, and for the first time in my life, I am beginning to feel at peace with my past. I wish it hadn't taken something so drastic, to stop me punishing myself for all my previous mistakes. But I am beyond grateful to be able to say that **I am finally moving on**.

The last few years of my life have been filled with so much frustration, believing that I am not where I should be because of all the time I've wasted being anxious and depressed. But the truth is that I am exactly where I should be. We face challenges every single day of our lives, and there will be times when they get the better of us, but all that matters is how we bounce back from it. Yes, I may have missed out on some opportunities up to this point, but I wholeheartedly believe that I am now ready to take the ones that are truly meant for me. You cannot change the past, only the future, and I am finally ready to make the people that I love proud. I believe life after cancer is all about setting your sights high, and aiming for things that your past self didn't believe were possible. I will continue to step out of my comfort zone: making my TikTok videos, starting my own business, recording my own podcast, and spreading my message, because I no longer see any limits to this one invaluable chance at life we get.

This is not some sort of unrealistic illusion; bad days will still come thick and fast, but the difference is that I know I'm prepared for them now. Knowing that I will never return to the person I once was gives me the pride I need to keep pushing through. Cancer will forever be a worry, and the chance of a relapse is always a possibility. But that only cements your reason even more to say, 'F it; I'll take that risk because I have nothing to lose.' So, this is your sign to get out there and take what is yours. I wish you all the happiness and success in the world, you truly deserve it. If a misfit like me can turn it around, you can too.

If this book has resonated with you, then please feel free to reach out to me on TikTok @GDchat, or on Instagram @gdchat_. I would love to hear everything about you conquering your chemotherapy and other treatments. Let's make the most of what little time we have in this beautiful world. Also, keep an eye out for my new podcast, *'I Wrote a Suicide Note,'* if I'm ever brave enough to finally start it. I hope to continue waffling about the past, present, and future worries of my chaotic brain. Always remember: a problem shared is a problem halved. And repeat after me: **'I cannot be stopped!'**

Printed in Great Britain
by Amazon